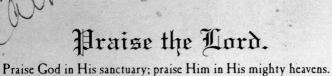

Praise the Lord.

Praise God in His sanctuary; praise Him in His mighty heavens.

Praise Him for His acts of power; praise Him for His surpassing greatness.

Praise Him with the sounding of the trumpet, praise Him with the harp and lyre,

praise Him with tambourine and dancing, praise Him with the strings and flute,

praise Him with the clash of cymbals, praise Him with resounding cymbals.

Let everything that has breath praise the Lord.

Praise the Lord.

Psalm 150

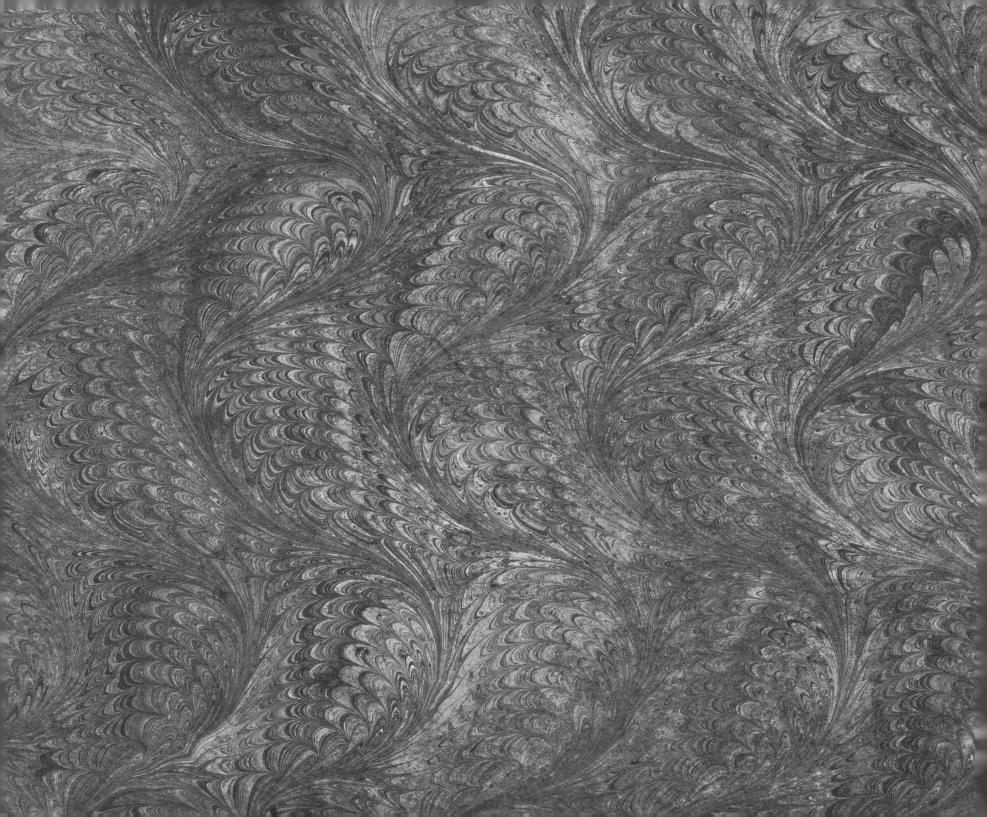

This Book

belongs to...

_____

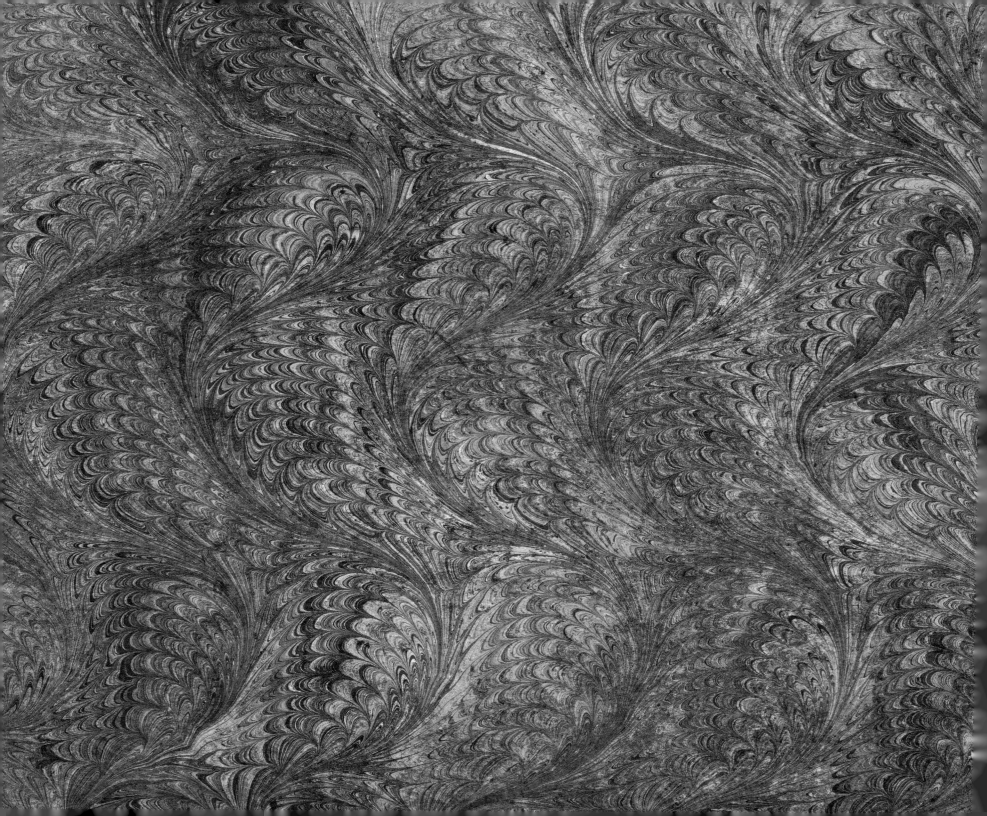

It was Christmas Eve, a time of celebration at the Wigglesworth home. There was so much excitement as the family waited for all their guests to arrive. Candles twinkled everywhere and the familiar fragrance of the Christmas tree filled the air.

The children were dressed in their favorite party clothes – Little Amy

all in pink, Chris Jr. looking just as handsome as his father,

and Mary Frances with her hair curled just right. Then there was Katherine,

the oldest, glowing in her purple gown. She looked so grown up.

The girls watched as Chris Jr. hovered around the Christmas tree.
He was delighted with all the beautiful packages and shook the largest ones
as he picked sweets off the tree's branches.

Family and friends began to arrive and fill the house with laughter.
The party had begun! The children danced joyfully and exchanged gifts with each
other. Even the parents joined in with a graceful waltz. It was a special night.

The children jumped and squealed with delight when Grandfather and Grandmother Wigglesworth arrived. Katherine loved them so much. They had just returned from a distant land and were anxious to tell everyone about the miracles God had done. They also brought many gifts, including dolls from different nations.

First, they brought out two large boxes, each wrapped in festive paper and tied with brightly colored ribbons and bows. Out of the first box came Harlequin and Columbine. What a cute pair they were as they twirled around on their toes. Next, surprisingly, a clown doll jumped out of the other box. Everyone laughed and clapped as he did somersaults all over the room.

From his big red bag, Grandfather Wigglesworth pulled out a toy drum for Chris Jr. He gave Little Amy a beautiful angel doll with shining wings. For Mary Frances, he had a special nativity ornament from Spain.

Before Grandfather Wigglesworth gave Katherine her gift, all the children begged for a story. He gathered them around and shared the greatest story of all – the story of Jesus. He told them how God sent His only son Jesus to be born in a manger, and that is why we celebrate Christmas. He also told them that Jesus died on a cross and rose again so that one day all who trust in Jesus can live forever with Him in heaven.

Luke 2:1-20

When Grandfather Wigglesworth finished, he gave Katherine her gift,
a most precious gift – his Bible. Katherine loved Jesus with all her heart
and she wanted to one day be a missionary just like her grandfather.

Mark 12:28-31

After the party ended and all the guests had left for home, Katherine snuggled into a big chair with her new Bible. As she read, she fell into a deep sleep and had a dream – *A Christmas Dream.*

Psalm 119:11-16

She dreamed of a strange battle, one that was taking place over her. Fly-like creatures with bulging red eyes and big web-like black wings began attacking her with one purpose in mind, to steal the Word of God out of her heart. She was so frightened, she didn't know what to do.

John 10:10

All of a sudden, Beelzebub, Lord of the Flies, appeared. How ugly he was!
He picked Katherine up and tossed her into the air to the other flies and
laughed at her feeble attempts to get away. There was no one
to help her and she felt all hope was gone.

Psalm 46:1-3

But then, in a blaze of glory, Michael the Archangel came to her rescue. He was magnificent, dressed all in white with a shining golden sword at his side. With him came the angelic hosts of heaven and a battle began.

Psalm 34:7

Throughout this extraordinary combat between the forces
of good and evil, Katherine remembered the promise in God's Word that
the battle is His and He will bring the victory. Beelzebub, no match for
the Lord's army, was banished back to his realm.

II Chronicles 20:15

Katherine then witnessed a beautiful celebration – angels dancing – angels everywhere, dancing and rejoicing because of Michael's victory.

I John 5:3-5

To her surprise, a golden chariot guided by two angels arrived and carried Katherine up into the clouds. "Where are they taking me?" she wondered. She would soon find out.

In what seemed to be a twinkling of an eye, she found herself in the most beautiful place she had ever seen. The joy she felt was indescribable. "Could this be heaven?" she thought.

I Corinthians 15:51-52

Different colored birds flew all around her. Even butterflies and
bumblebees joined in the celebration.

Psalm 148

Then there were the angels – little angels, big angels,

angels with bowls of incense.

It was a glorious place and the air was full with the fragrance of flowers.

At the sound of a trumpet, in walked Jesus to greet her. He welcomed Katherine into His Kingdom and invited her to sit next to Him on His throne.

Ephesians 2:6-10

All at once, many nations came to dance before Jesus. First, there were the Spanish dancers in bright red dresses.

Revelation 15:3-4

The Arabian dancers came next with flowing scarves. They moved so
gracefully as they rejoiced before their King.

Romans 5:1-2

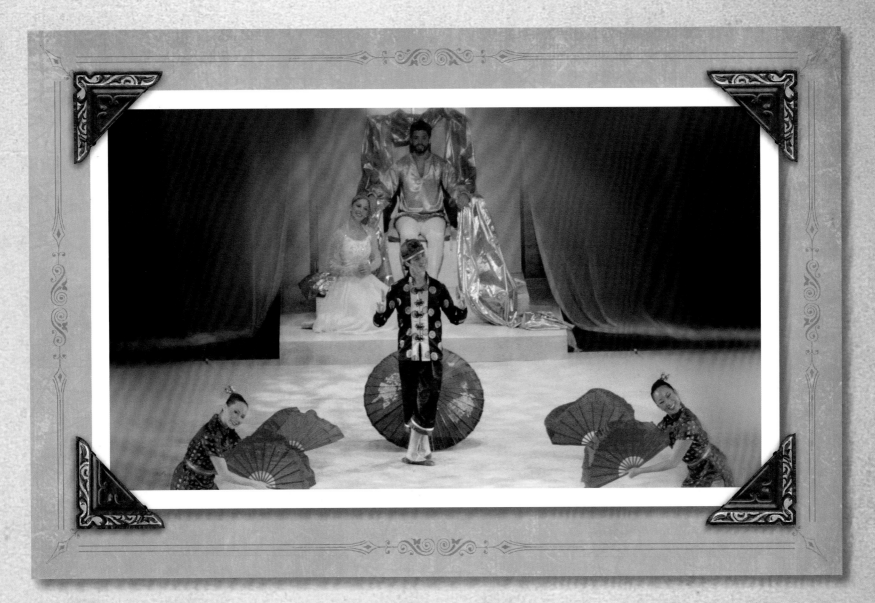

Entering with big fans and big smiles were the Chinese dancers, and Russian dancers

came jumping and spinning, joyfully giving thanks to their Maker.

Psalm 100

Next came the Ribbons of Righteousness dance. Pastel colored ribbons swirled everywhere - what a sight! The kids of the Kingdom followed, sliding in on bright colored rainbows, playing with rings of joy. Even their pigtails danced!

Malachi 4:2; Matthew 19:14

The Waltz of the Redeemed was one of pure beauty. With flower garlands in their hands, they bowed before the One who had granted them eternal life.

Psalm 107:1-3

Finally, it was Katherine's turn. Jesus took her hand and they danced

a beautiful pas de deux. How happy she was. She was dancing with Jesus!

Psalm 30:11-12

As she curtsied before Him, a host of angels bearing magnificent golden roses appeared. Soon angels were spinning and soaring all around her.

What a breathtaking celebration! All of heaven was rejoicing.

Then Jesus Himself placed the crown of life on Katherine's head.

James 1:12

On **Christmas morning,** Katherine awoke and found herself in the big chair. She recalled all the adventures of the night before – the victory Michael the Archangel had over Beelzebub and her journey into Heaven. She held her Bible close and on that day, that very special day, she came to know the real meaning of Christmas – that Jesus is the best gift of all.

John 3:16

Recognized in the international world
of ballet, Ballet Magnificat! is the benchmark
for professional Christian dance.

From the Kennedy Center in Washington, DC, to Singapore's historic Victoria Theater, thousands around the world have experienced Ballet Magnificat! With world-class dance, powerful performances and original ballets, Ballet Magnificat! touring companies deliver life-impacting experiences. Under the direction of Founder and Artistic Director Kathy Thibodeaux, Silver Medalist at the 1982 USA International Ballet Competition, Ballet Magnificat! has earned a reputation for excellence.

Ballet Magnificat! is dedicated to presenting the good news of Jesus Christ to the world. This multi-dimensional ministry is a major influence in the restoration of dance in the church and has spawned Christian dance troupes and schools around the world.

For more information, contact Ballet Magnificat!, 5406 I-55 North, Jackson, MS 39211 · 601.977.1001 · www.balletmagnificat.com

Keith and Kathy Thibodeaux

Ballet Magnificat! Executive Director and Artistic Director

Kathy stepped into the spotlight of the international dance world in 1982, winning a silver medal at the II USA International Ballet Competition. Against the advice of others, she expressed her faith in a dance to Sandi Patti's "We Shall Behold Him". Longing to see the art of dance restored to the church for the glory and honor of Jesus Christ, in 1986, Keith and Kathy founded Ballet Magnificat!, the world's premier Christian ballet company.

Keith is the former child entertainer best known as "Little Ricky" on the *I Love Lucy* television series. He went on to become drummer for the groundbreaking Christian rock band, David and the Giants, and later Executive Director of Ballet Magnificat!

Keith and Kathy make their home in the Jackson, Mississippi area where the Ballet Magnificat! studios are located. They have one daughter, Tara, married to former NBA player Bryce Drew.

Kathy had the vision for *A Christmas Dream* for several years, and in 2006 choreographed the ballet to celebrate the 20th Anniversary of Ballet Magnificat! Set in the Old South to the famous music of Tchaikovsky's *Nutcracker*, this was Ballet Magnificat!'s largest production ever, including over 150 dancers, 300 costumes, and innovative sets and choreography. The production included the professional companies, as well as students from the Ballet Magnificat! Professional Training Program and School of the Arts.

A Christmas Dream was first performed on December 15, 16, and 17, 2006, at Thalia Mara Hall in Jackson, Mississippi. It was during these performances that the pictures for this book were taken.

A Christmas Dream © 2006, 2007, Ballet Magnificat!
By Kathy Thibodeaux

ISBN #978-0-9799864-0-6
Published by Magnificat! Publishing Company, a division of Ballet Magnificat!, Jackson, MS 39211

A Christmas Dream Ballet
Choreography by Kathy Thibodeaux
Battle Scene Choreography by Jiri Sebastian Voborsky

Photography by Madel Perez,
Marion and Gary Silber, J. Mark Reed

Book Design: Imaginary Company
Vidal Blankenstein and Tyler Tadlock

Project Editor: Brenda Holden

Printed and bound by Friesens Corporation, Canada

www.balletmagnificat.com

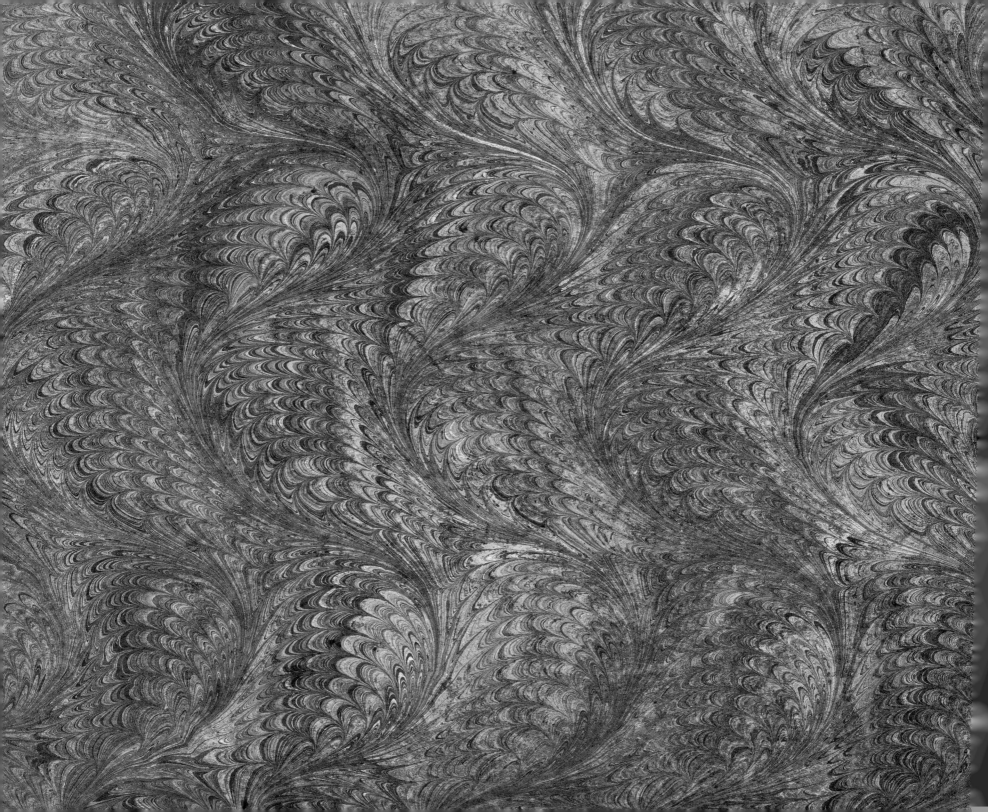